PR
LEA
· Quiz Book ·

FIFA WORLD CUP
Includes
2014 World Cup
questions

22 | 46
SEASONS | TEAMS

Compiled by a Welshman

Written in Scotland

Printed in England

Played all over the World

This edition first published in the UK in March 2015 by MyVoice Publishing

Copyright: © J S Williams

J S Williams asserts the moral right to be identified as the author of this work

Published by: MyVoice Publishing,

www.myvoicepublishing.co.uk

ISBN: 978-1-909359-50-5

 Threepoints Quiz

would like to welcome you to test your knowledge on the competition formed as the FA Premier League following the decision of clubs in the Football League First Division to break away from The Football League, which was originally founded in 1888, and take advantage of a lucrative television rights deal.

Television has played a major role in the history of the Premier League. The money from television rights has been vital in helping to create excellence both on and off the field. The League's decision to assign broadcasting rights to BSkyB in its very first season was at the time a radical decision, but one that has paid off. At the time pay television was an almost untested proposition in the UK market, as was charging fans to watch live televised football. However, a combination of Sky's strategy, the quality of Premier League football and the public's appetite for the game has seen the value of the Premier League's TV rights soar. The first Sky television rights agreement was worth £304 million over five seasons.]The next contract rose to £670 million over four seasons. The third contract was a £1.024 billion deal with BSkyB for the three seasons from 2001–02 to 2003–04.

The Premier League has since become the world's most watched association football league. It is the world's most lucrative football league in terms of revenue, with combined club revenues of €2.479 billion in 2009–10.

The Premier League deal is now worth £1 billion a year as of 2013–14, with BSkyB and BT Group securing the rights to broadcast 116 and 38 games respectively. The Premier League is the most-watched football league in the world, broadcast in 212 territories to 643 million homes and a potential TV audience of 4.7 billion people

All of the above has created a magnet for all clubs and players alike. The reward for any new club reaching the Premier League is an estimated £60 million for just one season. However the 38 game season results in despair for 3 clubs every year as the promotion and relegation places are fiercely competed for.

This book highlights all the clubs who have taken part in the Premier League including some who have completed just one season and never returned! In relation to the clubs any individual player who is fortunate enough to maintain a Premier League contract for just a few seasons will find himself propelled into pop star/actor status and of course personal financial security in a very short time, often at a very early age.

Whether alone or with friends, please enjoy attempting the possible 295 answers in this edition. Please agree to disagree and hopefully, by the end of the book, you will have enjoyed and learned something new and been surprised by the statistics created by the world's most famous football phenomenon....the Premier League!

Good luck

www.threepointsquiz.com

_ThreePoints Quiz

The 380 fixtures for the 2013–14 Premier League season were announced on 19 June 2013. The season started on Saturday 17 August 2013, and concluded on Sunday 11 May 2014. During the 2013–14 season, the Premier League used goal-line technology for the first time.

During the 2013–14 season, first place changed hands 25 times, compared to just four times during the 2012–13 season. That represented the most lead changes since the 2001–02 season – which had 29, the most ever. The championship was not decided until the final day of play for just the seventh time in league history. Manchester City won the league with a 2–0 victory over West Ham United on the final day, finishing with 86 points. In total, Manchester City led the league just 14 days throughout the season en route to their second championship in the last three seasons. The club scored 102 goals, one short of the record, while also conceding the second fewest goals in the league.

With two weeks to go, Liverpool looked certain to win the championship before they had a loss and a draw in two of their final three games. The team ended up in second place with 84 points. Chelsea came third, while perennial power and 2013 champions Manchester United had a disappointing season under new manager David Moyes (who was sacked in April) and finished seventh. It was their first finish outside the top three in Premier League history, and the first time they had not qualified for European football in 25 years. Southampton's eighth place finish and Everton's 72 points were club records. Sunderland, who were dead last on Christmas Day, rallied to avoid relegation. Norwich City, Fulham, and Cardiff City were the bottom three teams and were relegated to the Football League Championship.

Two teams (Manchester City and Liverpool) scored more than 100 goals for the first time in league history. The feat has only once been achieved before – by Chelsea in 2009–10. Luis Suárez easily won the golden boot for most goals with 31, ahead of teammate Daniel Sturridge who came second with 21 goals. Wojciech

Szczęsny of Arsenal and Petr Čech of Chelsea led the league with 16 clean sheets each. In a game against Southampton, Asmir Begovic became just the fifth goalkeeper in league history to score. Begovic's goal was also the fastest of the season, occurring just 12 seconds into the game.

Some notable facts about Season 2013-14......

Winners	Manchester City	86pts
Runners up	Liverpool	84pts
Relegated	Norwich City, Fulham, Cardiff City	
Top Scorer	Luis Suarez	31 goals
Best Goalkeeper	Peter Cech and Wojciech Szczesny 16 clean sheets)	

Biggest home win Manchester City 7 Norwich City 0

Biggest away win   Tottenham Hotspur 0 Liverpool 5

Highest scoring   Manchester City 6 Arsenal 3
Cardiff City 3 Liverpool 6

Final Table Season 2013-2014

		PLD	W	D	L	F	A		PTS
1	Manchester City (C)	38	27	5	6	102	37	+65	86
2	Liverpool	38	26	6	6	101	50	+51	84
3	Chelsea	38	25	7	6	71	27	+44	82
4	Arsenal	38	24	7	7	68	41	+27	79
5	Everton	38	21	9	8	61	39	+22	72
6	Tottenham Hotspur	38	21	6	11	55	51	+4	69
7	Manchester United	38	19	7	12	64	43	+21	64
8	Southampton	38	15	11	12	54	46	+8	56
9	Stoke City	38	13	11	14	45	52	−7	50
10	Newcastle United	38	15	4	19	43	59	−16	49
11	Crystal Palace	38	13	6	19	33	48	−15	45
12	Swansea City	38	11	9	18	54	54	0	42
13	West Ham United	38	11	7	20	40	51	−11	40
14	Sunderland	38	10	8	20	41	60	−19	38
15	Aston Villa	38	10	8	20	39	61	−22	38
16	Hull City	38	10	7	21	38	53	−15	37
17	West Bromwich Albion	38	7	15	16	43	59	−16	36
18	Norwich City (R)	38	8	9	21	28	62	−34	33
19	Fulham (R)	38	9	5	24	40	85	−45	32
20	Cardiff City (R)	38	7	9	22	32	74	−42	30

Quiz 1

1. In which year was the first ball kicked in the newly formed English Premier League?

2. How many teams played in the first Premier League season?

3. Which team won the first ever Premier League title?

4. Which team found themselves 10 points clear in January of the first ever Premier League and finally finished in 3rd place?

5. Who finished runners up in that first season which remains their highest finish position in the Premier League?

6. Name the Club, with a legendary and sometimes controversial Manager, who finished bottom of the very first completed Premier League season?

7. True or False? Newcastle United played in the first Premier League season.

8. Who finished highest in the first ever Premier League season - Arsenal or Sheffield Wednesday?

9. Who finished lower in the first Premier League season -Leeds United or Sheffield United?

10. Which Tottenham Hotspur striker finished top scorer in the first ever Premier League season with 22 goals?

Maximum score   **My/our score**

10

Quiz 2

1. In the 22 seasons of the Premier League, how many different teams have won the title? (number only)

2. Name the only player to have scored more than 200 goals in the Premier League?

3. Who was Manager of Arsenal in their first ever Premier League season?

4. In the completed 22 seasons of the Premier League, how many teams have played in every season? (number only)

5. How many top 3 positions have Manchester United achieved in the 22 completed seasons?

6. How many teams have only played just one season in the Premier League ?(number only)

7. How many different teams have secured at least one top three position in the 22 completed seasons?(number only)

8. Who has scored more goals in the Premier League, Ryan Giggs or Paul Scholes?

9. How many English Managers have managed to win the Premier League in the completed 22 seasons ?

10. Which Club was absent from the first Premier League season and then finished 3rd the following season at their first attempt?

Maximum score   **My/our score**

10

Quiz 3

1. Which Leeds United legend was their Manager when they were relegated from the Premier League in 2003-2004 season?

2. Which season did the Premier League start the season with 20 clubs for the first time instead of the original format of 22?

3. Name the 6 Clubs beginning with the letter "W" who have competed in the Premier League?

4. Did Michael Owen score more Premiership goals for Newcastle or Liverpool?

5. Fulham have just been relegated from the Premier League for the first time. How many seasons did they consecutively complete?

6. Which is the only Team in the Premier League to have been relegated on 4 occasions?

7. Who was Manager of Queens Park Rangers when they finished 5th in the very first Premier League season?

8. Who did Les Ferdinand score the most Premier League Goals for QPR, Newcastle or Tottenham ?

9. Have Birmingham City ever finished in the top ten of the Premier League in the 7 seasons they have been involved?

10. Who has spent the most seasons in the Premier League..... Derby County, Leicester City or Nottingham Forest?

Maximum score   **My/our score**

15

Quiz 4

1. West Bromwich Albion have completed 8 seasons in the Premier League. How many times have they been relegated?

2. Everton have been present in all 22 completed seasons. How many top ten finishes have they achieved?

3. Who, in London, has hosted the most seasons in the Premier League....... Fulham, Queens Park Rangers or Charlton Athletic?

4. The late Gary Speed played 535 games in the Premier league for Leeds, Everton, Newcastle and Bolton over a 17 year period. Which Club had his services for the longest time?

5. Did Darren Ferguson ever play a game for his Father at Manchester United in the Premier League?

6. Who scored more Premier League goals Thierry Henry or Robbie Fowler?

7. Can you name the 3 Clubs who have achieved just one top 3 finish in the 22 years of the Premier League?

8. How many different Clubs have played in the Premier League in its 22 year history?(number only)

9. Quiz 2, Question 6 asked "How many Teams have completed just one season in the Premier League and your answer should have been 5. Can you name the 5?

10. Which Team, on the south coast, has completed more seasons in the Premier League, Portsmouth or Southampton?

Maximum score

16

My/our score

Quiz 5

1. There are 7 Clubs which have completed all 22 seasons and therefore have earned points accordingly. Which Club is presently in 8th position of points earned in the Premier League?

2. What do Bradford City, Reading, Oldham, Hull City and Watford have in common regarding the Premier League?

3. What is the lowest number of points, resulting in relegation, achieved in one season of the Premier League? (number of points only)

4. Which Club has completed the most seasons in the Premier League, Leeds United, Bolton Wanderers or Middlesbrough?

5. Name the Club which has completed just 5 seasons in the Premier League, achieved one top 3 finish and been relegated 3 times ?

6. True or False ? Arsenal legend Ian Wright scored more than 100 Premier League goals

7. Queens Park Rangers have competed in just 6 Premier League seasons. How many top 10 finishes did they achieve?

8. Did Portsmouth ever achieve a top 10 finish in their 7 completed seasons in the Premier League?

9. Alan Shearer scored 260 Premier League goals in his unbelievable career. For which Club did he score the most, Blackburn Rovers or Newcastle United?

10. Who has scored more Premier League goals for Liverpool, Robbie Fowler, Steven Gerrard or Michael Owen ?

Maximum score   **My/our score**

10

Quiz 6

1. In the completed 22 seasons of the Premier League, who are the only 2 clubs who have achieved 22 top 10 finishes?

2. Who is Sheffield Wednesday`s top Premier League scorer, Mark Bright, Benito Carbone, Andy Booth or David Hirst?

3. Teddy Sheringham is Tottenham`s all time Premier League top scorer. Who lies in second place, Jermain Defoe or Robbie Keane?

4. Who is the top Premier League scorer for West Ham United, Paulo Di Canio, Carlton Cole or Trevor Sinclair?

5. Chris Sutton is Blackburn Rovers second highest ever Premier League goal scorer behind Alan Shearer. For which Club is he actually the highest Premier League scorer?

6. In the 22 completed seasons which club has had the highest number of top ten finishes, Aston Villa or Tottenham Hotspur?

7. Quiz 2 ,question 4 asked how many Clubs have competed in all 22 seasons and your answer should have been 7. Can you name them?

8. Who is Newcastle United`s second highest Premier League goal scorer behind Alan Shearer, ...Peter Beardsley or Andy Cole?

9. There are only 2 Clubs who can boast having three goal scorers who have scored more than 100 Premier League goals for the Club. Can you name the 2 Clubs and the six players?

10. Who is Aston Villa's top Premier League Goal scorer Dion Dublin, Gabriel Agbonlahor or Dwight Yorke ?

Maximum score   **My/our score**

24

17

Quiz 7

1. Who has completed the most seasons in the Premier League, Ipswich Town or Norwich city?

2. Who has achieved the highest number of top 10 finishes in the Premier League, Leicester City or Derby County?

3. Who has been relegated the most times from the Premier League, Leeds United, Manchester City or Sheffield Wednesday?

4. Quiz 4 question 8 asked how many different teams have played in the Premier League in its 22 year history. Your answer should have been 46. Which Club were the 46th to appear in the Premier League in season 2013-2014?

5. Who were the 45th Club to achieve Premier League status playing in the 2011-2012 season?

6. Jan Aage Fjortoft scored 6 goals for Barnsley in their one and only appearance in the Premier League making him their 3rd highest scorer. For which Club is Jan the highest Premier League scorer?

7. Who has scored the most Premier League goals for Everton, Tim Cahill, Kevin Campbell or Duncan Ferguson?

8. Which team has completed the most seasons in the Premier League...Blackburn Rovers, Manchester City or Newcastle United?

9. Who has spent the most seasons in the Premier League Blackburn Rovers, Manchester City or Southampton?

10. Aston Villa`s Darren Bent spent 2 complete seasons at Charlton Athletic, Sunderland and Tottenham Hotspur. For which Club did he score the most Premier League goals?

Maximum score

My/our score

10

Quiz 8

1. Who did Carlos Tevez scored more Premier League goals for, Manchester City or Manchester United?

2. Who has completed the most seasons in the 22 Premier League seasons from the North East, Middlesbrough, Newcastle or Sunderland ?

3. Who was Manager of Aston Villa when they finished runners up in the first ever Premier League season 1992-93?

4. Eric Cantona scored 15 Premier League goals in the very first Premier League season 1992-93. Were they scored for Leeds United, Manchester United or both?

5. How many different Premiership Clubs has Andy Cole played for ?(number only)

6. How many top 3 finishes have Newcastle United achieved in the Premier League?

7. Who was Manager of Nottingham Forest when they had their only top 3 finish in season 1994-95 ?

8. Leicester City`s most successful time in the Premier League was their 4 consecutive top 10 finishes from 1996-97 to 1999-2000 seasons. Who was their Manager throughout that period?

9. Darren Bent is the 2nd highest goal scorer for 2 Premier League Clubs. Can you name them?

10. Did Paul Gascoigne ever play in the Premier League ?

Maximum score

My/our score

11

Quiz 9

1. How many Players have scored 30 goals or more in a single Premier League season?(number only)

2. Swansea City achieved their highest ever finish of 9th place in season 2012-13. Which Club achieved their highest ever Premier League position of 9th place in season 2013-2014?

3. There are 23 players who have scored more than 100 Premier League goals. Can you name the 6 who have scored them all for just one club?

4. Which FA Cup final scorer, and ex Manager of Aberdeen, managed Chelsea in the first season of the Premier League in 1992-1993?

5. The top three scorers for Leeds United in the Premier League are Harry Kewell, Mark Viduka and Rod Wallace. Which one of the three has scored the most for the Club?

6. The top three scorers for Coventry City in the Premier League are Dion Dublin, Peter Ndlovu and Noel Whelan. Which one of the three has scored the most for the Club?

7. The top three scorers for Derby County in the Premier League are Malcolm Christie, Dean Sturridge and Paulo Wanchope. Which one of the three has scored the most for the Club?

8. Who has had the most top 10 finishes in the Premier League in its 22 year history, Chelsea or Aston Villa?

9. How many teams have been relegated 3 times or more from the Premier League? (number only)

10. Included in the question above is a Club who were relegated in 1992-93, 1994-95, 1997-98 and 2004-05 making them the only Premier League team to have been relegated on 4 occasions. Name the Club?

Maximum score

15

My/our score

WELCOMES BACK ....

BURNLEY FC

TO THE

PREMIER LEAGUE

GOOD LUCK FOR THE COMING 2014 -2015 SEASON

1. What year did Burnley`s last play in the Premier League ?

2. What is Burnley`s highest finish position in the Premier League?

3. Which Player is Burnley`s top Premier League goal scorer?

WELCOMES BACK ....

LEICESTER CITY

TO THE

PREMIER LEAGUE

GOOD LUCK FOR THE COMING 2014 -2015 SEASON

1.   What year did Leicester city last play in the
     Premier League ?

2.   What is Leicester city's highest finish position in
     the Premier League?

3.   Which Player is Leicester city's top Premier
     League goal scorer?

ITS HALF TIME........WE HOPE YOU ARE ENJOYING.....

HOWEVER.....AFTER SURVIVAL SUNDAY   11TH
MAY 2014   THIS BOOK WILL BE OFFICIALLY BE
OUT OF DATE... THE PREMIER LEAGUE WILL HAVE
COMPLETED ITS 23RD SEASON.... SO DO NOT GET
INTO ANY ARGUMENTS AFTER THAT DATE....JUST
LOOK OUT FOR......

SEE INSIDE BACK COVER

WELCOMES BACK ....

QUEENS PARK RANGERS
TO THE
PREMIER LEAGUE

GOOD LUCK FOR THE COMING 2014 -2015 SEASON

1. What year did QPR last play in the Premier League ?

2. What is QPR`s highest finish position in the Premier League?

3. Which Player is QPRs top Premier League goal scorer?

27

Quiz 10

1. Quiz 4 question 9 asked..."How many Teams have completed just one season in the Premier League and your answer should have been 5. Can you name the 5?" Your answer should have been Barnsley, Burnley, Blackpool ,Cardiff City and Swindon Town. Can you name the 6 Managers (2 for Cardiff City) who were involved?

2. Who has completed the most seasons in the Premier League – Derby County or Nottingham Forest?

3. Which 2 Premier League Clubs did Steve Coppell manage?

4. Who has completed the most seasons in the Premier League- Fulham, Leeds United or Southampton?

5. The top 3 Premier League goal scorers for Middlesbrough are Juninho, Hamilton Ricard and Mark Viduka. Which one is their top scorer with 31 goals?

6. Premier League season 1997-98 finished with three players as joint top scorers with 18 goals- Dion Dublin, Michael Owen and Chris Sutton. Which 3 clubs were represented by these players?

7. Premier League season 1998-99 also finished with three players as joint top scorers also with 18 goals- Dwight Yorke, Michael Owen and Jimmy Floyd Hasselbaink. Which 3 clubs were represented by these players?

8. Who has been the top scorer for a Premier League season on the more occasions- Thierry Henry or Alan Shearer?

9. Did Gary Lineker ever play in the Premier League?

10. Southampton played in the first ever Premier League season and stayed there for 13 seasons. Who was their Manager when they were relegated in 2004 -05?

**Maximum
score**

20

My/our score

Quiz 11

1. Name the top 3 goal scorers in the 22 completed seasons of the Premier League?

2. Quiz 2 Question 5 asked .."How many top 3 finishes have Manchester United achieved in the completed 22 seasons?" Your answer should have been 21. Arsenal lie in 2nd place with how many top 3 finishes?

3. Did Sheffield United complete 1, 2 or 3 seasons in the Premier League?

4. Which Team has achieved the more top 3 finishes in the Premier League, Chelsea or Liverpool ?

5. Quiz 4 question 7 stated there are 3 Clubs who have achieved just one top 3 finish. Your answer should have been Aston Villa(2nd) 1992-93, Norwich City(3rd) 1992-93 and Leeds United(3rd) 1999-2000 . Can you name the 3 Managers who were in charge ?

6. Who has achieved the most top 3 finishes in the Premier League- Blackburn Rovers or Newcastle United ?

7. True or False ? Everton and Tottenham Hotspur have never finished in the top 3 of the Premier League.

8. The top 3 top 3 finishers in the Premier League are Manchester United, Arsenal and Chelsea with 38 top 3 finishes between them. Who lies in 4th place with 7 top 3 finishes?

9. Name the 3 players who have played the highest number of Premier League games?

10. Which 3 Premier League Clubs have the highest ground capacities?

Maximum score   **My/our score**

18

Quiz 12

The following 4 pages list all 45 Premier League Clubs in descending order of how many Premier League seasons they have completed. Fill in the spaces next to the Club with the number of seasons ....(3 done for you in each quiz)

Team	*Premier League seasons*
Arsenal	22
Aston Villa	
Chelsea	
Everton	
Liverpool	
Manchester United	22
Tottenham Hotspur	
Newcastle United	
West Ham United	
Blackburn Rovers	
Manchester City	17

Maximum score

My/our score

8

32

Same again.....fill in the number of completed seasons.....

Team	Premier League Seasons
Southampton	15
Middlesbrough	
Bolton Wanderers	
Fulham	
Sunderland	
Leeds United	12
Coventry City	
Charlton Athletic	
Leicester City	
Sheffield Wednesday	
Wimbledon	8

Maximum score

8

My/our score

Still in descending order fill in the number of completed seasons for Teams 23 to 33 in the Premier League....

Teams	Premier League seasons
West Bromwich Albion	8
Wigan Athletic	
Birmingham City	
Derby County	
Portsmouth	
Norwich City	7
Queens Park Rangers	
Stoke City	
Ipswich Town	
Nottingham Forest	
Crystal Palace	5

Maximum score

8

My/our score

And last but not least…..please insert the number of seasons completed by these Clubs in 34th to 46th positions in the Premier League….

Teams	Premier League Seasons
Wolves	4
Sheffield United	
Swansea City	
Bradford City	
Hull City	
Oldham Athletic	
Reading	2
Watford	
Barnsley	
Blackpool	
Burnley	
Cardiff City	
Swindon Town	1

Maximum score	**My/our score**
10	

Quiz 16

1. Quiz 2 Question 7 asked how many Teams have achieved a 3rd place or higher in the Premier league and your answer should have been 11.   Premier League winners Manchester United, Blackburn Rovers, Arsenal, Chelsea and Manchester City make five. Can you name the other 6?

2. Quiz 5 Question 3 asked "What is the lowest number of points, resulting in relegation, achieved in one season of the Premier League?(number of points only) Your answer should have been 11points. Name the Team who achieved this in season 2007-08?

3. Quiz 8 Question 5 asked "How many different Premiership Clubs has Andy Cole played for?(number only)"..... Your answer should have been 7......Can you name them?

4. Quiz 9 Question 1 asked "How many Players have scored 30 goals or more in a single Premier League season?(number only)"....Your answer should have been 7. Can you name them?

5. Did Les Ferdinand score for 4, 5 or 6 different Premier League clubs?

6. Quiz 9 Question 9 asked "How many teams have been relegated 3 times or more from the Premier League? (number only)"....Your answer should have been 9 ..... Can you name them?

7. You have previously named the 7 Teams who have completed all 22 seasons of the Premier League, Manchester United, Arsenal, Chelsea, Liverpool, Everton, Tottenham Hotspur and Aston Villa. Name the 2 other Clubs who have never been relegated from the Premier League?

8. Who is the highest scoring Defender in the Premier League scoring 38 goals?

9. Excluding Harry Redknapp, name the five other Managers who have managed 4 different Clubs in the Premier League?

10. Teddy Sheringham scored 147 Premier League goals in his career. Name the 4 Clubs he scored those Premier League goals for.

Maximum score   **My/our score**

42

Quiz 17

1. Which Tottenham Hotspur striker became the 21st player to score 100 Premier League goals in season 2011-2012?

2. Mark Viduka is Leeds United`s highest ever Premier League goal scorer. For which Club is he also the 3rd highest Premier League scorer?

3. Who is the oldest? Ryan Giggs or Paul Scholes.

4. Which Premier League Club has the highest number of letters in its full name with 22 letters?

5. Which Premier League Club has the shortest number of letters in its full name?

6. Emile Heskey played for 5 Premier League Clubs between 1994 and 2012. Can you name them?

7. Name the 4 Premier League Clubs who can boast to be geographically the most North, South, East and West in the United Kingdom?

8. Who was Manager of Charlton Athletic when they were relegated from the Premier League in 2006-2007?

9. Who was Manager who took Hull City up into the Premier League for season 2008-2009 and was relegated with them after 2 seasons in 2009-2010?

10. Oldham Athletic were present in the first two seasons of the Premier League in 1992-93 and 1993-94. Who was their Manager at that time?

Maximum score

17

My/our score

Quiz 18

1. Can you name the 3 Managers who have managed both Blackburn Rovers and Liverpool in the Premier League?

2. Quiz 16 Question 7 asked who are the 2 teams who have never been relegated from the Premier League and your answer should have been Stoke City and Swansea City. Who out of the 2 has completed the most seasons?

3. When Blackburn Rovers won the Premier League title in 1994-1995 who was their goalkeeper?

4. Arsenal and Chelsea have both one the Premier League on 3 occasions....True or False?

5. Who has been relegated the most times from the Premier League....Sheffield Wednesday, Burnley or West Ham United?

6. Who has completed the most seasons in the Premier League, Nottingham Forest or Queens Park Rangers?

7. What have Blackburn Rovers and Manchester City achieved regarding the Premier league that no other Team has managed?

8. Quiz 7 question 1 asked of fierce rivals Norwich City and Ipswich Town " Who has had the most seasons in the Premier League" and your answer should have been Norwich. Which one has been relegated the most times?

9. Manchester United won the Premier League in 1995-1996 and 1996-1997 with Liverpool and Arsenal finishing in 3rd place respectively. Which Club finished 2nd on both occasions?

10. Leeds United and Leicester City have not played in the Premier League since they were relegated together. In which season were they relegated?

Maximum score   **My/our score**

12

1. Quiz 18 question 6 asked "Who has completed the most seasons in the Premier League, Nottingham Forest or Queens Park Rangers?" and your answer should have been QPR. Which team has been relegated on the more occasions?

2. Which two Clubs did Kevin Keegan manage in the Premier League?

3. Which Club has been relegated on more occasions from the Premier League....Burnley, Reading or West Bromwich Albion?

4. Sheffield Wednesday and Wimbledon have almost identical records in the Premier League completing 8 seasons, achieving 3 top ten finishes and suffering 1 relegation. Which Team achieved the highest position of 6th in the Premier League?

5. Birmingham City, Derby County, Portsmouth and Norwich City have all completed 7 seasons in the Premier League. Which one has only been relegated once?

6. Quiz 6 question 1 asked…. "In the completed 22 seasons of the Premier League, who are the only 2 clubs who have achieved 22 top 10 finishes?" Your answer should have been Liverpool and Manchester United. Who lies in 3rd place with 21 out 22 top ten finishes?

7. Who has had the more top ten finishes in the Premier League Chelsea or Tottenham?

8. Who has had the more top ten finishes in the Premier League…. Aston Villa or Everton?

9. Derby County had two consecutive top ten finishes in seasons 1997-98 and 1998-99. Who was their Manager at that time?

10. Name the only Scotsman to have managed Tottenham Hotspur in their 22 years of the Premier League?

Maximum score

My/our score

11

Quiz 20

1. Fulham`s highest finish in the Premier League was 7th in season 2007-08. Who was their Manager at that time?

2. Name the 7 Manchester United players who have gone on to manage a Premier League Club?

3. Who was Charlton Athletics Manager for their 8 year stretch in the Premier League 1998-2006?

4. Who was Manager of Middlesbrough when they were relegated from the Premier League in 2009?

5. Who last completed a season in the Premier League Sheffield United or Sheffield Wednesday?

6. Which two teams were relegated from the Premier League after its second season in 1993-1994 and have never played in the Premier League since?

7. Which Team has completed just 2 seasons in the Premier League 1999-2000 and 2006-2007 and finished bottom on both occasions?

8. Which two teams were in the first Premier League first season 1992-1993, completed 8 seasons, were relegated together in season 1999-2000 and have never played in the Premier League since?

9. Aston Villa are the most successful club from Birmingham, competing in all 22 Premier League seasons. But who lies in 4th place in the 2nd city for the least number of completed seasons, Birmingham City, West Bromwich Albion or Wolverhampton Wanderers?

10. Steven Fletcher, currently at Sunderland, is top scorer for 2 other Premier League Clubs …Can you name them?

Maximum score

My/our score

19

Quiz 21

All questions are World Cup based but have a Premier League connection.

1. Bobby Moore was England `s 1966 winning World Cup captain. What was his middle name?

2. Which 3 Premier League players started the 2014 World Cup Final?

3. Which 3 Premier League players came on as a substitute in the 2014 World Cup Final?

4. Name the Premier League player who scored 4 goals in the 2014 World Cup Tournament?

5. Name the only player in England`s 2014 World Cup squad who was NOT a Premier League player?

6. Name the 3 Swansea City players who were involved in the 2014 World Cup Tournament?

7. Name the Premier League player who scored 3 goals in the Tournament?

8. Name the 4 Premier League players who scored 2 goals each in the Tournament?

9. The first World Cup Finals after the Premier League was formed were in the United States of America in 1994. The final is the only one not to have taken place in a Capital City. Which City hosted the 1994 World Cup final?

10. Roy Hodgson was England`s Manager for the 2014 World Cup Finals. Can you name the 4 Premier League Clubs Roy has managed in the Premier League?

Maximum score

22

FIFA WORLD CUP
Brasil

My/our score

Answers

Quiz 1 1. 1992/93 2. 22 3. Manchester United 4. Norwich City 5. Aston Villa 6. Nottingham Forest 7. False 8. Sheffield Wednesday 9. Leeds United 10. Teddy Sheringham

Quiz 2 1. 5 2. Alan Shearer 3 George Graham 4. 7 5. 20 6. 5 7. 11 8. Ryan Giggs 107 Paul Scholes 106 9. None 10. Newcastle United

Quiz 3 1. Eddie Gray 2. 1995/96 3. West Bromwich Albion, West Ham United, Wolverhampton Wanderers, Wigan Athletic, Watford, Wimbledon 4. Liverpool 5.13 6. Crystal Palace 7. Gerry Francis 8. QPR 9. Yes 9th 2009/10 10. Leicester City

Quiz 4 1. 3 2.11 3. Fulham 4. Newcastle United 5. Yes Manchester Utd 92/93 6. Thierry Henry 7. Aston Villa (92/93) Leeds United (99/00), Norwich City (92/93), 8. 46 9. Barnsley, Blackpool, Burnley, Cardiff City, Swindon Town, 10. Southampton

Quiz 5 1. Newcastle United 2. Played 2 seasons only 3. 11 points 4. Middlesbrough 5. Nottingham Forest 6. True 7. 3 8. Yes – twice 9. Newcastle United 10. Robbie Fowler

Quiz 6 1. Liverpool and Manchester Utd 2. Mark Bright   3 Robbie Keane 4. Paulo Di Canio 5. Norwich City 6. Tottenham Hotspur 7. Manchester Utd, Arsenal, Chelsea, Liverpool, Everton, Tottenham, Aston Villa. 8 Peter Beardsley 9. Manchester United ,Giggs , Scholes and Rooney Liverpool Fowler, Owen and Gerrard 10. Gabriel Agbonlahor

Quiz 7 1. 5 2. Leicester City 3. Manchester City 4 Cardiff City 5. Swansea City 6. Swindon Town 7. Duncan Ferguson 8. Newcastle 20 Blackburn 18 Man city 17 9. Blackburn 18 Manchester City 17, Southampton 15 10. Sunderland

QUIZ 8 1. Manchester City 2. Newcastle 3. Ron Atkinson   4. Leeds United 6 goals, Manchester united 9 5. 7 6. 4 7. Frank

Clark 8. Martin O Neil 9. Charlton Athletic and Sunderland
10. Yes Middlesbrough 98/99 Everton 2000/2002

QUIZ 9 1. 7 2. Stoke City 3. Henry & Wright Arsenal, Giggs &
Scholes Man Utd, Le Tissier Southampton, Drogba Chelsea 4.
Ian Porterfield 5. Mark Viduka 6 Dion Dublin 7. Dean Sturridge
8 Chelsea 9. 9 10. Crystal Palace

QUIZ 10 1. Danny Wilson, Owen Coyle, Ian Holloway,(Malky
Mackay & Ole Gunnar Solskjaer)John Gorman 2. Derby
County 3. Crystal Palace and Reading 4. Southampton. 5.
Hamilton Ricard 6. Coventry City, Liverpool, Blackburn Rovers
7. Manchester Utd, Liverpool, Leeds Utd. 8. Thierry Henry 9. No
10. Harry Redknapp

QUIZ 11 1. Alan Shearer 260, Andy Cole 187, Thierry Henry 174
2. 12 3. 3 4. Chelsea 5. Ron Atkinson, Mike Walker, Howard
Wilkinson, 6. Newcastle Utd. 7. True. 8. Liverpool 9. Ryan
Giggs(632), Frank Lampard (577), David James (572) 10. Man
Utd (75,797) Arsenal (60,361) Newcastle Utd (52,339)

QUIZ 12 1. Aston Villa 22, Chelsea 22, Everton 22, Liverpool 22,
Tottenham Hotspur 22, Newcastle Utd 20, West Ham Utd 19
Blackburn Rovers 18,

QUIZ 13 Southampton 14, Bolton Wanderers 13, Leeds Utd 12,
Fulham 12, Coventry City 9, Charlton Athletic 8, Leicester City 8,
Sheffield Wednesday 8

QUIZ 14 Birmingham city 7,Derby County 7, Portsmouth 7,
West Bromwich Albion 7 , Queens Park Rangers 6, Ipswich
Town 5, Nottingham Forest 5, Stoke city 5,

QUIZ 15 Sheffield United 3, Bradford City 2, Hull City 2, Oldham
Athletic 2, Reading 2,Watford 2, Barnsley 1, Blackpool 1,
Burnley 1, Swindon Town 1

QUIZ 16 1 Aston Villa, Leeds United, Liverpool, Newcastle
United, Norwich City, Nottingham Forest 2. Derby County
3. Newcastle United, Manchester United, Blackburn
Rovers, Fulham, Manchester City, Portsmouth, Sunderland
4. Alan Shearer, Andy Cole, Thierry Henry, Kevin Phillips,
Cristiano Ronaldo, Robin Van Persie,Luis Suarez 5. 6 (QPR,

Newcastle, Spurs, West Ham, Leicester, Bolton) 6. Crystal Palace, Birmingham City,Bolton Wanderers, Leicester City, Middlesbrough, Sunderland, West Brom, Nottingham Forest, Norwich City 7. Stoke City, Swansea City 8. David Unsworth 9. Graeme Souness (Liverpool, Blackburn, Southampton, Newcastle), Ron Atkinson (Villa, Coventry, Sheffield Wednesday, Nottingham Forest), Sam Allardyce (Bolton, Newcastle, Blackburn, West Ham,) Roy Hodgson(Blackburn, Fulham, Liverpool, West Brom).Mark Hughes (Blackburn, Fulham, Man City, QPR) 10. Tottenham, Manchester United, Portsmouth, West Ham

QUIZ 17 1 Jermain Defoe 2 Middlesbrough 3 Ryan Giggs (10 months older) 4 Wolverhampton Wanderers (22 letters) 5 Fulham(6 letters) 6 Leicester City, Liverpool, Birmingham City, Wigan Athletic, Aston Villa 7 Newcastle United, Southampton, Norwich City, Swansea City 8 Alan Pardew 9 Phil Brown 10 Joe Royle

QUIZ 18 1 Kenny Dalglish, Graeme Souness, Roy Hodgson 2 Stoke City 3 Tim Flowers 4 True 5 West Ham Utd 6 QPR (6) , Forest (5) 7 Been Champions and been relegated. 8 Norwich City 9 Newcastle Utd 10 2003-2004

QUIZ 19 1 Nottingham Forest 2 Newcastle Utd, Manchester City 3 West Bromwich Albion 4. Wimbledon (1993/94) 5 Portsmouth 6 Arsenal 7 Chelsea 8 Aston Villa 9 Jim Smith 10 George Graham

QUIZ 20 1 Roy Hodgson 2 Gordon Strachan, Steve Bruce, Roy Keane, Bryan Robson,Paul Ince,Mark Hughes, Ole Gunnar Solksjaer 3 Alan Curbishley 4 Gareth Southgate 5 Sheffield United (2006-2007) 6 Swindon Town and Oldham Athletic 7 Watford 8 Sheffield Wednesday and Wimbledon 9 Wolverhampton Wanderers (4 seasons) 10 Burnley (8)and Wolves (22)

QUIZ 21 1. Chelsea 2 Mezut Ozil, Martin Demichellis, Pablo Zabaletta 3. Andre Schurle, Sergio Aguero, Per Mertesacker 4 Robin Van Persie 5 Fraser Forster (Celtic) 6 Michel Vorm (Holland) Jonathan De Guzman (Holland) Wilfried Bony (Ivory

Coast) 7. Andre Schurle 8. Oscar (Chelsea) David Luiz (Chelsea) Wilfried Bony (Swansea City) Luis Suarez (Liverpool) 9 Rose Bowl, Pasedena, California 10. Blackburn Rovers, Fulham, Liverpool, West Bromwich Albion

Burnley`s only season in the Premier League was 2009-2010 when they finished 18th . Their top Premier League is Steven Fletcher with 8 goals.

Leicester City last played in the Premier League in 2003-2004. Their highest finish is 8th in 1999-2000. Their joint top Premier League goal scorers are Emile Heskey & Muzzy Izzet with 33 goals

Queen Park Rangers last played in the Premier League in 2012-2013. Their highest finish is 5th in 1992-1993. Their top Premier League Goal scorer is Les Ferdinand with 60 goals

22 46 gives you 21 quizzes with 315 answers !

Whether you completed this book religiously alone or just had fun with family and friends down your local we are sure you are now far more informed regarding the most exciting Football league in the world!

Whether you managed less than 50 correct answers or managed to achieve 100 or the dizzy heights of over 150 correct answers we hope you had fun along the way.

If you managed to achieve more than 200 correct answers then perhaps you should be getting out a bit more and getting a real life ! If you achieved more than 250 correct answers then maybe you should be applying for the next Premier League Manager position that becomes available.

On the subject of Managers we wish all the best to Ole Gunnar Solskjaer, Chris Hughton and Felix Magath who were all relegated with Cardiff City, Norwich City and Fulham respectively.

We wish the best of luck also to Nigel Pearson, Sean Dyche and Harry Redknapp who will embark on their respective Premier League campaigns with Leicester City, Burnley and Queens Park Rangers in August 2014.

The 2014-2015 Season kicks off in mid August 2014 and will
be beamed around the World to over 190 Countries. Who will

win the 23rd playing of the Premier League and who will be the unlucky 3 who will be relegated on Survival Sunday in May 2015 ?

Enjoy the season everybody !

COMING SOON.....